4—

Just

Loons

Just Loons

A WILDLIFE WATCHER'S GUIDE

Text by Alan Hutchinson
Photography by Bill Silliker, Jr.

WILLOW CREEK PRESS

MINOCQUA, WISCONSIN

Published by Willow Creek Press

P.O. Box 147, Minocqua, Wisconsin 54548

Edited by Andrea Donner

Designed by Patricia Bickner Linder

ISBN 1-57223-687-6

Originally published in 1998; original ISBN 1-57223-146-7
Library of Congress Cataloging-in-Publication Data (1998):
Hutchinson, Alan.
        Just loons : a wildlife watcher's guide / by Alan Hutchinson : photography by Bill Silliker, Jr.
            p.   cm.
        ISBN 1-57223-146-7
        1. Common loon. 2. Bird watching.   I. Title.
    QL696.G33H88   1998
    598.4'42—dc21   98-15958
                                                                       CIP

Printed in Canada

Acknowledgments

We wish to thank a group of very special people who deserve special recognition. This is a large group—so large that it is impossible to mention each by name. This group is comprised of all the many, caring people across this land who give untiringly of themselves for the conservation of loons. They include biologists, rangers, wardens, teachers, researchers, naturalists, photographers, writers, and innumerable volunteers. They include the many conservation organizations, their staffs and their members who provide support. They include all who donate to their states' nongame wildlife programs through tax checkoffs or conservation license plates. These are the people who give their time, their money, their efforts, and their hearts to the conservation of the common loon. They are the ones shouldering the burden. We send our deepest appreciation and gratitude to each of you included in that large yet special group, and encourage all others who read this to join with them in the conservation of this marvelous creature of our natural world— the common loon.

Author's Dedication

To my family . . .
To my wife, Terri, and son, Jon, for their love and
support in sustaining me in my pursuits. And to my
parents for the direction they gave my life and for the
encouragement they gave me to pursue my dreams.

Photographer's Dedication

Wildlife photographers need not only encouragement
and support, they also require subjects with which
to work. So I'd like to thank my parents for the
encouragement they've always given me, my wife for
all of her support, and the loons on these pages
for permitting me to capture on film some of the
magic moments of their lives.

Table of Contents

Introduction by David C. Evers, Ph.D.

Canoeing through a disorienting early morning mist your lost feelings are dispelled by a loon's distant wail signaling all is well. Soon, fortune befalls, and you share an unexpected close encounter with a loon silently surfacing by your side. Your reaction reflects your connection: a quiet sense of happiness and appreciation is reciprocated with curiosity as the loon relaxes at the water's surface, head held high, and softly hooting to convey its satisfaction. A startling swat at a mosquito and your encounter is met with a bit more apprehension and the loon simply disappears. Timeless aquatic encounters creating countless stories prolong the bond that we have with loons.

I have been fortunate to spend much of my professional life interacting with loons. They certainly are a captivating inhabitant of this earth. Loons have much to teach us about balance and nature's harmony. Native peoples shared many of these lessons through stories, and these stories endure even today, reflecting our special connection with this bird. It is this connection

that commands our vigilance as loons are exposed to ever-growing threats from human encroachment. In summer, loons in the U.S. and southern Canada must compete for space on increasingly crowded waters. Boating activity, the popularity of personal watercraft, improper use and disposal of lead fishing tackle and line, and our tendency to favor building shoreline houses, continue to impact annual breeding success. In autumn, adding to the normal dangers of migration are human-induced impacts such as botulism outbreaks along the lower Great Lakes (an ecological reflection of a cast of introduced species). In the western U.S, severely elevated mercury levels threaten lakes that serve as important migratory staging areas. Along both the eastern and western coasts, wintering loons are faced with one of their harshest threats – oil spills. Add to all of these a globally-increasing atmospheric deposition of mercury, creating population-level risks for loons in some parts of their breeding range, and you can understand the compelling need to continue close surveillance. After all, if the loon cannot survive in its watery environment, how can we?

With this in mind, *Just Loons* is the sort of written story that reminds us of the important and timeless connection we have with this remarkable bird. It includes simple descriptions of what loons are all about using many new scientific findings. We now have a very good idea of the loon's life history and its needs — reflecting over a decade of intensive research with banded individuals. *Just Loons* also provides a wonderful blueprint for interacting with loons through an understanding of their breeding needs and interpretation of their body language. Most importantly, the pictorial story presented in these pages fully captures the beauty, elegance and individuality of this bird. It is a species that commands great respect by virtue of its singular grace and uncommon awareness of its surroundings. Enjoying the company of loons by respecting the space they require will go far in maintaining healthy populations in a world of shrinking wilderness.

David C. Evers
26 December 2002

David Evers is the Executive Director and Senior Biologist for BioDiversity Research Institute, an ecologically-minded nonprofit based in Falmouth, Maine. This group conducts original research and monitoring projects across North America with an emphasis on using birds as indicators of aquatic integrity. To learn more about this group visit www.BRILoon.org.

The Wonder of Loons

The lake was a glassy calm with a slight mist rising from its surface; a perfect morning for a quiet canoe paddle to enjoy the sunrise and see what we could see. My Dad and I, up and out early, glided along the shores and inlets of this beautiful Maine lake, paddling slowly and silently to enjoy the sights, sounds and smells of that early June morning.

The small island with its stand of stately white pines had always been a favorite spot for us to explore and enjoy. Today would prove the same.

A short paddle stroke put us into a quiet glide around the island's point. There before us as we rounded the point, a pair of loons dove and fished in the shallows. Our silent approach gave them

but a moment's pause before they returned to their fishing. As we sat quiet and still, snapping a few photos now and then, the loons moved closer to us, diving and feeding between short pauses to rest and preen. They barely seemed concerned with our presence.

We shared that corner of the lake for half an hour, the sense of wonder growing in us with each passing minute that we spent in the presence of these marvelous creatures. We felt so thankful to be a part of their natural world and to share those moments. As brief as those moments were, they stay with me, as I know they still do with my Dad.

As we left our loon companions, we pondered what was at work that morning that made our presence so acceptable to them. We posed innumerable questions about these birds and about the life of loons in general. The pursuit of answers to those questions has led to this book—a book about common loons and the joys of

seeking, finding and watching them. It is our aim to aid in these pursuits, while also providing an understanding of the natural history, habits, and habitat needs of the common loon, the loon most often seen on the lakes and ponds and along the coasts of North America.

The common loon holds a special place in the hearts and minds of people. It is a symbol of wilderness and of special wild places yet untarnished. It is a touchstone to the natural world and to our past and, perhaps, to things unknown. Could that be why the call of the loon provokes such awe and mystery?

In the Presence of Loons

What is it about being in the presence of loons that most excites you? Why is it that the voice of a distant loon makes you yearn to see it up close? How is it that your soul is stirred when a loon calls out across a still, backwoods pond at midnight?

Do you long for something that the loon represents? Perhaps the sight of a loon evokes subliminal memories of the wild—of life in a wilderness once called the New World.

As our planet grows ever more populated and civilization increasingly shrinks the wilderness, the loon symbolizes something special, something many feel we have nearly lost. The presence of loons somehow brands a place as pristine and labels a lake as tranquil, a spot to treasure when we seek relief from the pressures of a technological society. And because loons prefer places where few people go, and require lakes that have less motorboats, jet skis and other trappings, the presence of loons signifies a chance for a simpler, quieter life for those who seek the experiences our forefathers enjoyed when they went to the north-woods, to the wilderness, to the wild.

More of us are going to those woods these days. And as we do we sometimes endanger the very birds that proclaim that wilderness still exists. We must take care that our use of the places that these precious, ancient birds call home does not lead to their decline, or worse, to their extinction.

This book is intended to help those who seek the enjoyment of loon watching learn how to behave in their presence. As you read, you will learn that loons already face enough challenges from the modern world without the added stress of those who might inadvertently "love them to death."

In these pages you will learn how to watch loons without interfering in their lives. You will find out how to read loon body language and to understand what they're saying when they call out in their different voices. And you will learn how to photograph loons for great results while using low impact methods. You, too, can be accepted in the presence of loons.

You will also learn how you can help make the world a safer place for these birds, so that future generations may wonder at their beauty, and get a chance to feel that indefinable sensation when a loon calls out during the dark of night.

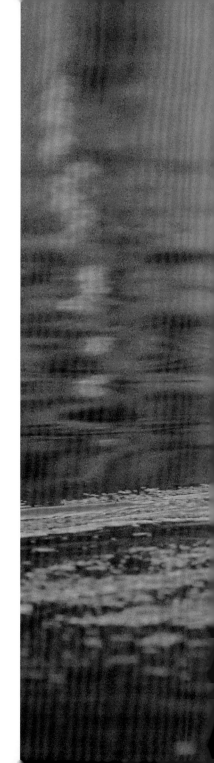

Loons at a Glance

Common loon – those haunting mysterious birds of northwoods lakes and ponds. They appear each spring at ancestral nesting sites from parts unknown, unerring in their timing, to announce another burst of spring. They entertain us with their flights and antics. They awe us with their otherworldly calls throughout the summer nights. They go about their private business of secretive nesting and then tease us with periodic glimpses of their chicks as they grow through the summer months.

They worry us as we wonder if their chicks will survive: Will they grow enough to fly before the lakes freeze hard again? And if so, will the chicks survive the harsh new world they face, and return some other spring to renew our hope and joy?

As its name implies, the common loon *(Gavia immer)* is the most common species of loon in North America. It is also, therefore, the one most people encounter. Much of what you learn about the common loon, however, applies to the other four species of loons you could see in your travels.

▶ Common loons appear each spring at ancestral nesting lakes and ponds.

When you learn more about common loons, your appreciation and enjoyment of them will only grow. And as your knowledge about loons grows, your questioning and curiosity will also grow as you realize just how complex their lives are, and how much we still do not know about these special birds.

What are these magnificent creatures that come and go as the seasons change? What challenges do they encounter in their daily lives? What impacts them during the seasons of change and migration? And what explains the meaning of their calls and antics that we hear and witness? The following quick guide will help you find the answers to these and other frequently asked questions about loons.

What kinds of loons are there?

There are five species of loons in the world: The common loon *(Gavia immer)*; the yellow-billed loon *(Gavia adamsii)*; the red-throated loon *(Gavia stellata)*; the Pacific loon *(Gavia pacifica)*; and the Arctic loon *(Gavia arctica)*. All occur in North America, but the common loon is the only species that nests in the United States with the exception of Alaska.

When do common loons nest?

Loons return to their nesting lakes as soon as the ice disappears. Egg laying begins in May or early June in latitudes of Maine and Minnesota, but several weeks later in the extreme North. They begin to leave the lakes in autumn, beginning in September. Some will stay until ice on the lakes forces them south.

Where do common loons build their nests?

Loons require a safe, secluded site to nest. Because they need to swim to the nest, it is typically at the water's edge, only inches above the water level. The site is often on an island or small peninsula with quick access to deep water for a diving escape.

How many young do they have?

An average clutch contains two eggs. Some only have one. Rarely, three are laid. A day or two separates the laying of each egg, the result being a day or two between the hatching of each chick.

Which parent incubates the eggs?

Both adults take turns sitting on the eggs. Generally an equal effort, one parent may spend more time on the nest. Incubation lasts on average 27-29 days.

When do the chicks leave the nest?

The chicks leave the nest within 12 to 24 hours of hatching, often as soon as their down is dry. They may not touch land again until they nest as adults several years later.

When do the chicks first fly?

Young loons take their first flight at about three months old, at the end of their first summer. Learning how to fly is a gradual process, and proficiency for these large and heavy birds only comes with time.

How fast do chicks grow?

Chicks grow from just a few ounces at hatching to a weight of 6 to 8 pounds, close to their adult weight, in just three months.

When do common loon chicks start to look like adults?

Loons gain their full adult plumage when 2 years old. A chick's first set of feathers, which replace the down by their first autumn, look like the adult's winter plumage. In the spring, when adults gain their breeding plumage again, young birds continue to wear this more drab look of winter.

How big are common loons?

Loons grow to a wide array of sizes. Common loons range in weight from 7 to 16.5 pounds. The average depends on where the loon lives. Their wing span approaches 60 inches, and their body length nearly 3 feet. Males average 20 percent larger than females.

Why do common loons look different from winter to summer?

Feathers wear out just like clothes. If they were not replaced, loons could not fly, would not be waterproof, and would freeze during winter. Loons replace their feathers twice a year in a process called molting. One complete change of feathers occurs just before the spring migration. A second partial change begins at the end of summer and continues through fall migration.

◀ *This adult loon photographed in the ocean is molting into its winter plumage.*

▼ *As fall approaches, the loon on the left has begun to molt.*

How long do loons live?

Loons may live to be 25 to 30 years old, or more. Like all species of wildlife, the mortality rate of young in the first year or two is much higher than when it becomes an established breeder.

What do common loons need for habitat? Loons nest on fresh-water lakes and ponds. They generally require a quiet body of water in a remote locale with an adequate food supply for nesting success. Loons that are not nesting often remain in coastal waters or may frequent lakes and ponds in more developed areas that have higher boat traffic. Loons winter in coastal waters that do not freeze.

What is the range of the common loon? Common loons are northern nesters. Their breeding range extends from northern Canada to the tier of United States just south of the Canadian border, and from the Atlantic to Pacific coasts. Their migration is concentrated along the coasts but loons might be seen in spring or fall throughout North America. They winter on the Pacific, Atlantic and Gulf coasts.

How high and fast do loons fly? Loons have been reported flying more than 60 miles per hour, with one report in excess of 90 mph. Their wings beat at a rate of 3 to 4 beats per second. They have been reported to fly at altitudes of 1,500 to 2,700 meters above sea level when migrating over land, yet commonly are seen as low as just a foot or two above the water's surface.

Do loons spend much time on land?

Loons have been called "feathered fish" because they swim so well. They spend perhaps 96 percent of their life on water, touching land only at birth, during mating, when nesting, or when sick. Swimming is natural to young loons. They swim within hours of hatching and begin to dive when only a few days old.

How deep can loons dive?

The average dive lasts less than a minute. The maximum time a loon can stay underwater is about three minutes. There are reports of loons diving to depths of more than 150 feet. Most dives are rather shallow, usually less than 30 feet. Loons propel themselves with their feet when diving.

Do common loons migrate?

All loons must migrate. They need to leave their nesting lakes before they freeze. They may migrate from a few to more than a thousand miles between breeding and wintering areas, depending on where they spend the summer.

What do loons do in winter?

Loons spend the winter in ice-free coastal waters. They start to arrive in October and begin to leave in March. Loons winter across a broad range, from Alaska to Mexico on the Pacific Coast, from Newfoundland to Florida on the Atlantic Coast, and from Florida to Mexico on the Gulf Coast.

How do loons pick a mate?

Loons court their mates each spring on their nesting lakes. The courtship rituals, performed on the water, are not flashy affairs but build a bond between the pair that holds them together as they raise young. More dramatic territorial displays occur through the chick rearing period and strengthen these bonds.

Do common loons mate for life?

Loons are monogamous, meaning they typically choose and stay with just one partner each year. It was once believed that loons stayed with the same mate throughout life, but recent research indicates that partner changes, from year to year, are not uncommon.

What do loons eat?

Fish make up the primary source of food for loons, with crayfish, snails, dragonfly nymphs and other aquatic invertebrates being additional favorites. Crabs become an important part of their winter diet. Loons can swallow food underwater, as it is caught. Larger or spiny catches are brought to the surface first.

How many common loons are there?

There are an estimated half a million common loons across their range. The best estimates come from the lower 48 states where loon populations are the smallest and are therefore easier to count. The estimates for these states are about 21,000 birds. Canada and Alaska account for the rest.

Are loons endangered?

Common loons are not listed as Endangered or Threatened Species under either the U.S. or Canadian Endangered Species Acts. That reflects the relative health and large population size of the common loon across its entire range. It is a species of conservation concern, however, especially in the lower 48 states where its range has shrunk and populations are small. It has been listed as Endangered and Threatened within the borders of some states, and as a species of "special" or "management" concern in others.

CHAPTER TWO

Definition of a Loon

How would you describe a loon to someone who had never seen or heard one? What characteristics most capture the essence of a loon? What aspects of this bird make it truly unique among living things?

Such questions are worth exploring, for the answers may hold more than you'd expect. What you might find within your answers are insights about loons that would be missed at first glance, insights as to how the loon fits within the world around it.

What defines a loon? Asking yourself that question sharpens your eye to observation and brings about a deeper, more inquisitive way of wildlife watching. In this way, you will grow in your understanding and enjoyment of your time in the presence of loons.

A strong case can be made that, above all else, loons are defined by where they live—their watery homes. Loons are so perfectly designed for an aquatic life that they have been called "feathered fish." Their shape, their colors, their weight,

◀ *Loons are perfectly designed for an aquatic life.*

even their bones and skeleton, have all evolved toward one overriding purpose: the creation of an almost perfect design for life on the water.

The Body of a Loon

A loon's shape is an example of streamlining at its best. The near perfection of its form can be most appreciated when the loon is viewed head-on. From that vantage, you can see how the bill, which looks so sharp and pointed in silhouette, is actually quite broad and sturdy. You see how gracefully this stout bill blends into a surprisingly wide, stout head. You also then see how the head, in turn, blends seamlessly into the loon's long, broad body.

The shape of a loon presents a smooth and streamlined transition from head to tail, ending with the legs and feet protruding from the rear. The legs and feet fall too far back to support the loon in walking but are perfectly positioned to serve as powerful thrusters, similar to propellers on the world's fastest, most advanced submarines. Engineers designing submarines would do well to study the design of loons—the end result of millions of years of successful evolution.

The Eyes

The head-on view provides a look at another fascinating facet of a loon's anatomy: the eyes. Loons have strikingly colored crimson red eyes. While the color alone is enough to draw your attention to their eyes, there is a more compelling aspect that you will notice after time. Loons,

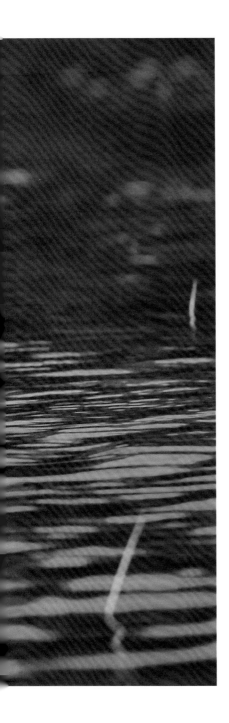

contrary to the behavior of many birds, will make direct eye contact with you and will watch you as you are watching them.

They are able to do this because of the position of their eyes. Many birds, such as ducks, geese, swans, grouse, and songbirds have their eyes on the sides of their heads. With such a design these birds see primarily to the sides, but can also see in the periphery: forward, backward, and all around—360-degree vision! That's a neat trick, and quite an advantage for animals that must always be on the lookout for predators hunting them as an easy meal. That design, however, eliminates the ability to focus both eyes together on the same object. Such birds, therefore, cannot judge distance very accurately.

Loons, on the other hand, like most animals that exist by hunting, are less concerned with what may be behind them. They need their vision pointed forward to gain a strong perspective of

depth and distance and a strong focus to aid in the accuracy of the hunt. Imagine the skill, coordination and athletic ability required of a loon in chasing and catching a swimming, fleeing fish. The design of their eyes makes this possible. The eyes of the loon tell you that this bird is a hunter.

The positioning of their eyes also permits loons to gaze into our eyes. Why they choose to engage us with eye-to-eye contact is a mystery. Sometimes they may have concern as they watch us and worry about our presence. But many times it seems that they stare at us for no reason other than curiosity. It is at those times, when their vision locks on yours, that you begin to feel a different sense about this bird that you're watching.

A Study in Camouflage

The colors and patterns of the common loon's feathers provide another way to help define them. Loons are dark on the top and light on the

bottom. What do these striking patterns of black and white tell us? Interestingly, this is a characteristic found in many birds that live on water. These are features designed for stealth and safety.

For a fish beneath the surface on the lookout for predators intent on making it a meal, the loon's white belly blends almost invisibly with the surface of the water as the fish looks up toward the light-colored sky.

This camouflage also helps protect the loon from predators that may be hunting it from below. Both snapping turtles and large fish predate on

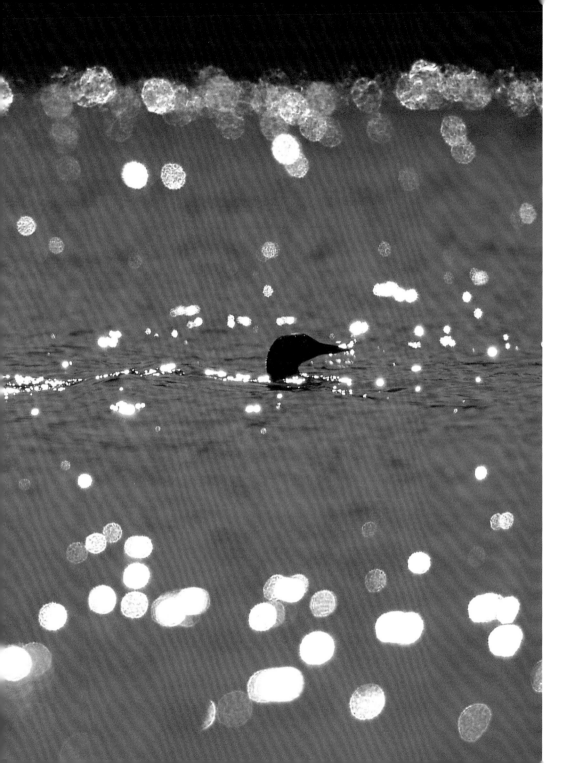

◀ *The pattern and colors of the common loon's feathers help it blend with its habitat.*

loons, and they are especially threatening to the smaller young. During winter on the coastal waters, sharks also view loons as a potential meal.

But danger not only lurks below, there are also threats from above. Eagles present a constant threat. So what better way to survive than to blend into the background when viewed from above as well? Their dark backs do that perfectly when set against the surface of the water. It appears that the contrasting patterns of black and white spots and streaks on the loon's back and sides aid in this deception as they mimic the shimmering light reflecting from the surface of a lake.

A Skeleton for Survival

The skeleton of the loon is intriguing as well. Consider that the most overriding characteristics that distinguish birds are their evolutionary adaptations for flight. Lightness of weight is a key factor in the achievement of flight. Loons, in contrast to many of their feathered cousins, balanced their divergent evolutionary route to less weight against their needs to dive and to swim while submerged.

Lightness would certainly help loons stay afloat, but if light, loons would struggle to stay beneath the surface and would never succeed in catching fish. How did loons overcome this problem?

The lightness that birds need to permit flight has been partly achieved through the evolution of hollow bones. The bones of most animals are filled with marrow, the source of red blood cell production. Birds evolved an anatomy of certain bones being hollow and marrowless, with chambers connected by a network of air sacs that are in turn connected to their lungs.

Loons, however, have forsaken that adaptation

and have more solid than hollow bones. The added weight gives the loon's body a density almost exactly that of water, resulting in neutral buoyancy! That provides a great advantage for a diving bird, as it gives unparalleled ease in diving and staying submerged. With such ease loons expend little energy to stay underwater, another benefit to survival.

You can see that the design characteristics one bird would need for flight do not match the

▲ *Loons balance an adaptation for flight with a design for diving.*

▶ *Its nearly neutral buoyancy enables this loon to swim low in the water as it peers below the surface for food.*

◀ Designed for the water, the common loon struggles greatly when on land, as this one does to get to its nest.

features needed for a life of diving underwater. Birds that can both fly and dive have thus needed to perform a delicate evolutionary balancing act.

Loons have pushed this balance to the edge. Their evolutionary adaptations go about as far as can be toward the diving mode without giving up the ability to fly. Much more of a shift, and the common loon might well become the penguin of the North: a beautiful swimmer that has forsaken flight.

These special attributes of loons have been noticed and admired whenever and wherever people have come into their presence. The various names given the loon attest to that. In most parts of the world, the birds North Americans know as loons are called "divers." Our common loon is also known as the "great northern diver," an apt description.

What's In a Name

The name "loon" was bestowed by early European settlers to North America and is believed to be based on a Scandinavian word for "clumsy," to describe the loon's difficulties moving about on land. The name "diver" seems much more appropriate, reflecting the strength of the bird's evolutionary design rather than a limitation that affects it during only a small part of its existence.

Native Americans, too, had their own names for this bird, each again being descriptive of its strengths that they admired so, such as its bravery, its call and its mysterious nature.

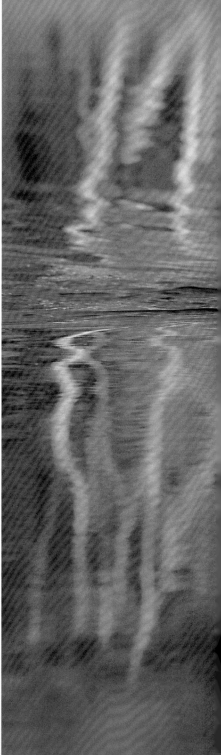

CHAPTER THREE

How to Find Loons:
Their Haunts and Habitats

How do you find loons to watch? There are three answers to this question: location, location, and location! Loons live within a specific geographic range. They move within that range according to seasonal patterns, choosing different types of habitats that meet their seasonal requirements. And they live at key places within these special habitats as dictated by their behavioral traits, as well as by their needs.

Knowing both when and where to look are the keys to success in finding loons. Your knowledge of four things will aid you in finding loons to enjoy: 1) The loon's geographic range; 2) Their travels through the seasons; 3) The habitats that they need and seek out; and 4) How they behave while in each habitat.

This chapter will give you the information you need to piece together the puzzle of a loon's life through the seasons. As your knowledge and understanding grow, so too will your chances of finding loons, and your appreciation of what you see.

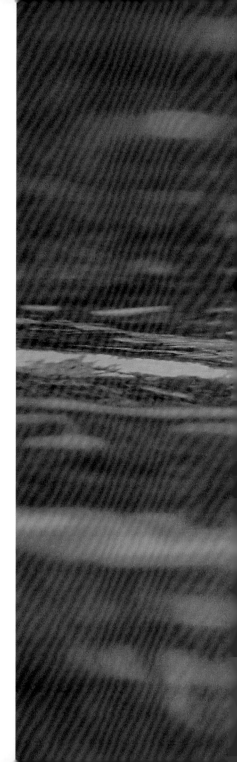

A few words of caution: loons are most vulnerable when they nest and as they rear their chicks on inland lakes and ponds in the summer. Since summer is the time when most people frequent lakes, that's when they see the most loons. It is also the most exciting time to watch loons, as they are active and vocal, as well as perhaps having chicks with them. But as you look for loons during summer, remember how critical

▶ *Thoughtful loon watchers allow a loon guarding its territory the space that it deserves.*

and sensitive the nesting period is for them, a time when any human presence can be most damaging. Whether loons are establishing nests, incubating eggs or raising their young, your approach can do the greatest of harm if not done with care and understanding.

Nesting Range

Common loons nest on northern lakes and ponds of adequate size and type across a broad swath of Canada and the northern United States, from the Atlantic to the Pacific coasts. They nest on lakes adjacent to the New England and Canadian Maritime coasts, on lakes scattered across three thousand miles of the North American continent, to lakes along Alaskan shores.

Your best chance to find loons is to search out suitable nesting lakes within the forested regions of their range. These birds are typically found on lakes associated with the great northern forests; they truly are a bird of the northwoods. The smaller lakes and potholes of the northern prairie country are not good places to look for loons. Loons also do not nest in saltwater habitats, probably for several reasons. A major one is that the changing tides would severely restrict a loon's ability to swim to the edge of its nest.

The northern tier of the United States marks the southern boundary of their present nesting range. In the East, Massachusetts and New York represent the southern edge.

The few birds now nesting in Massachusetts are actually recent returnees, and they provide an encouraging sign for the long-term health of loon populations. Historically, common loons nested into Connecticut and even in Pennsylvania. Loss of habitat from lakeshore development and disturbance by people led to their disappearance from those regions. Increased awareness by people using those lakes and improved knowledge and conservation programs are now beginning to reverse this trend.

You will encounter nesting loons more readily as you proceed north through their range into New Hampshire, Maine, northern New York—especially the Adirondacks region—New Brunswick and Quebec.

NESTING RANGE
WINTER RANGE

▶ *Always be alert to loon "body language." This loon lowered its head as another loon approached its nest.*

In the Midwest, common loons reach the southern limit of their breeding grounds in Michigan, Wisconsin, and Minnesota. To the north, their nesting range extends far into Ontario, then follows a northern curve into Manitoba, Saskatchewan and Alberta before dropping south again, following the forest lands of the continental divide into British Columbia and pushing far north and west into Alaska.

Common loons nest sporadically and locally through the northern tier of the far western United States. Similar to their experience in the East, loons once ranged much further south, even reaching into California.

The northern edge of the nesting range for the common loon follows an arc across the northern part of Canada and Alaska, roughly approximating the treeline. To the far north, as open tundra replaces the forest, others of the five species of loons become the more prevalent nesters.

Nesting Habitat

Loons seek out certain lakes and ponds to call home, the ones that satisfy their basic requirements. While much remains unknown about what characteristics make one lake more attractive than another to a loon, certain things that researchers do know can help you in your quest for loons to watch.

The first thing to remember is that a lake must have a large enough open stretch for a loon to use to become airborne. Like an overloaded airplane, a common loon needs a long runway of open water to gain enough speed to lift off. A loon "runs" across the water while beating its wings furiously to get enough lift to leave the surface.

To provide a good nesting site, a lake must also have an ample supply of fish of the right size and species. Some shallow lakes have no fish at all

because they freeze solid during winter. Others have no fish because of the nature of the water chemistry. Acid rain is unfortunately adding some former loon nesting lakes to that list, as their waters become increasingly polluted.

A lake that has fish must offer enough abundance to feed a family of loons. And those fish must be readily available for a loon to catch. Loons favor lakes with productive shallow waters and with clear visibility. A large, deep and dark lake populated only by fish species that live in the depths offers little for a loon.

Nesting lakes must also provide safe places to build nests and raise young. Islands, isolated peninsulas, and islets within channels in marshy coves or stream mouths provide ideal nesting habitat for loons. They furnish safe havens from predators such as raccoons, foxes, coyotes and

◀ *The colors and patterns of the loon's feathers also provide excellent camouflage while on the nest.*

skunks hungry for a meal of fresh eggs or hoping for an easy opportunity to catch an adult loon, so vulnerable while on the nest.

Shelter is as important as safety when loons choose a nesting lake. Both the nests and young of loons need shelter from strong prevailing winds and waves common along exposed shorelines.

Look for loons first at lakes with coves, bays, islands and marshy inlets. Lakes with straight shorelines, exposed to wind and waves, are less likely to be used for nesting. Check carefully, however, as you evaluate a lake's potential for loons. Many large lakes that may at first seem "un-loonlike" may harbor small areas offering just the right sheltering protection for a pair or two of nesting loons.

Finally, consider the size of the surface area as you search a lake or pond for loons. While common loons have nested on bodies of water as small as ten acres, most lakes adequate for loon nesting average fifty acres or more.

Lakes with larger surface areas broken up by coves, islands and peninsulas might provide habitat for more than one nesting pair of loons. Loons establish well defined territories that they defend against encroachment from other loons.

Lakes with many such hidden places that have adequate feeding waters nearby are good places to look for loons.

The haunting calls loons make while on their nesting lakes provide another valuable tool for you to use as you seek them out. A later chapter in this book describes the meaning of these various calls. Understanding what you hear should fine-tune your loon watching ability.

Winter Haunts

Loons leave their northern nesting grounds as fall approaches and the lakes begin to freeze. They fly to the coasts: Atlantic, Pacific, and Gulf of Mexico, where they spend the winter.

The range of common loons in winter spans thousands of miles from north to south. On the Atlantic, loons winter from Newfoundland all the way to the Florida Keys and into the Gulf of Mexico to just beyond the Mexico–Texas border.

The loon's Pacific winter range extends an even greater distance, from the Aleutian islands all along the Canadian and United States coasts and that of Baja California, in Mexico. The rare ability to adapt to such a wide range of conditions, from the ice and freezing ocean storms of the North Atlantic to the tropical conditions of Florida and Mexico, evidences the marvels of design and adaptability of this bird.

Loons usually don't linger inland on the migratory journey, but move quickly to their choice of coastal waters once they decide to leave their summer lake homes. This trait leaves little chance to predictably see loons during fall migration.

The one exception may be offered by the loons that nest in the midwestern states and to the north in Canada. Birds from this summer range migrate to the Gulf of Mexico by way of the Great Lakes and the major rivers of the Midwest. It is

well worth searching in that region of the United States during both the spring and fall migrations, as places exist there to see loons on a fairly regular basis.

Although common loons range so far and wide in winter, that does not make them so easy to find. Loons spend much time alone as they disperse during migration. Families break up. Even mated pairs do not stay together.

Approach finding loons in winter just as you

▲ *As fall approaches, a loon chick nears adult size and can fish for itself.*

would in the summer: base your search on habitat. Within their wide expanse of winter range, loons seek out certain types of areas for their winter homes. Such locations, just as during the summer, must provide the right mix of the things that a loon needs to survive. In the winter, that primarily involves food.

A dependable source of food is essential to a loon's survival. This becomes especially true during the harsh cold of winter. Their winter foods, primarily fish and crabs, must be readily available. It should come as no surprise to learn that loons most often frequent productive, food-rich shorelines in the winter months, typically in waters of no more than thirty feet in depth. Shallow waters near the mouths of tidal rivers, where currents and adjacent marshes make the areas rich in food, make great places to start your winter search for loons.

Without the vulnerable chicks or nests to protect, shelter becomes less important. Loons often choose to winter along coasts exposed to the most violent of winter storms. They are so well adapted to aquatic life that they don't seek shelter from these storms, but instead turn to the open sea. They swim away from the dangers of waves crashing on the shore to ride out the storm and the driving sleet and rain, howling winds and waves that tower fifty feet or more. After the storm has passed, they come back near shore to resume their search for food.

▼ *Loons gather briefly before the fall migration to the sea.*

When searching for loons at this time of year, remember that they change to drab colors that blend well with the winter seas. They also rarely call during winter, and since they seldom fly now as well, don't count on either of these behaviors to reveal their presence.

Although loons usually feed alone throughout the day, they may gather in loose flocks as evening approaches. Look for these aggregations at dusk and at dawn.

Also scan the edges of flocks of other waterfowl: loons frequently like to associate with eiders, scoters, old squaws or grebes, and will spend time feeding along the edges of those flocks.

Do Some Homework

Seek out and talk with people and groups near your home who may have local knowledge about loons. Nature groups, outdoor outing clubs, federal, state or local wildlife refuges, Audubon chapters and other bird watching groups are excellent places to make contact with people who are willing to share information with others interested in loons and their conservation.

Also try using topographic maps, coastal charts and other land classification information for the area you have an interest in. Such information is available for all areas of the United States and Canada, usually from a government agency, often at a public library or from bookstores. They will provide you with knowledge on the location of water bodies and their size, shape, depth, shoreline characteristics and degree of human development, and perhaps even of other degradations to them. Then use your knowledge about the habitat requirements and behavior of loons and apply it as you study your maps and other information on your area of interest.

Draw up a list of the locations where you think loons might find suitable habitat. Then visit and

◀ *Loons sometimes surface nearby when you least expect them.*

explore those sites and you'll learn a great deal from what you find there. Don't be surprised or discouraged if you don't find loons; knowing where not to find them is valuable information as well. It often takes multiple visits to a site inhabited by loons to verify their presence. Ask yourself why you find them in some seemingly suitable places and not in others. What patterns begin to emerge from what you find? The answers will guide you in future searches.

Also look for a guide to wildlife viewing areas specific to the state or province where you live or plan to visit. Many good ones are available. They often give excellent advice about where to find various wildlife, including loons.

Keep in mind that those guides won't list all the places where you can find loons. And they often don't even list the best ones. Some land owners or wildlife managers may not want to overwhelm certain areas with too many people through publicity of an especially sensitive spot. And some areas are yet to be discovered. If you find such a place to watch loons, treat it with special care yourself. Develop your own information about the best sites and then build relationships with those who own or manage those sites. Not only will that help you to enjoy loon watching at such special places, but it will also help the loons.

Some Final Tips

Loons traditionally choose and use the same areas for many years. Once you have found a location that loons frequent, you can almost count on finding them there later in that season or during the same season the following year.

Loons often return to the same nest site, and should that prove to be unsuitable, they will likely

◀ A quiet slow approach in a canoe provides a good way to enjoy loon watching.

nest nearby on the same pond or lake. They also return to the same winter haunts. Such locations can provide hours of fascinating loon watching entertainment year after year.

The importance of the right habitat for sustaining loons cannot be overstated. Once you have found those special spots, work with others nearby to conserve them for the special value that they provide.

CHAPTER FOUR
The Family Life of the Loon

Spring comes slowly to the lakes of the great northern forests of North America. The ice that has capped them through the winter may be up to three feet thick. Another two or three feet of compact snow may rest atop the ice, and snow as deep as six feet may rest in the surrounding woods. But when the lengthening days and warming sun finally break winter's grasp, spring arrives quickly. And with the spring a flourish comes to nature, rejuvenated with the prospect of another cycle of birth, of life, of growth.

The waters of northern lakes do not open gradually. Winter only begrudgingly lets go. Yet when the ice does disappear, it happens with a quickness that can startle, sometimes even occurring overnight. And when it does, do not be surprised to finds loons swimming there the next day.

The instinctual urge of loons to travel north and once again seek out ancestral nesting lakes is a powerful and driving force that awakens with the first hint of spring. Loons start to stir in their winter homes as early as February and March. By

◀ *Loons arrive as soon as the ice recedes from their summer homes.*

▶ *A loon lands on its breeding lake.*

mid-March, loons begin leaving Florida, Mexico and other southern portions of their winter range. By the middle of April, spring migration peaks along the shores of the mid-Atlantic states and in California. Inland flocks of up to three hundred loons may start to gather on the larger lakes, reservoirs, and rivers of the Midwest. By May, this northern surge has reached New York, New England and the Canadian Maritimes in the East, Oregon, Washington and British Columbia in the West. Individual birds, pairs, or small groups

then start to break away from the coast and scatter inland, aiming for the nesting lakes that they call home.

These returning birds scout and probe ahead, testing to see if the ice has gone. They can cover hundreds of miles a day in these pursuits. When not on flying searches, they spend the day on large bodies of waters, coastal bays or lakes that have thawed, feeding and waiting in anticipation of spring's arrival farther north. When spring finally does arrive they go, eager to move on, hopeful to find their home lake ice-free, but ready to wait again at another more northern place.

The nesting range of the loon spans a thousand miles from south to north and reaches to the Arctic Circle. This results in a great spread in time between when the most southern and most

northern pairs begin to nest. Loons in southern Minnesota and Maine may already be sitting on eggs while their more Arctic cousins still wait patiently for the ice to leave their nesting lakes.

Mating Rituals

How and when the male and female rejoin after a winter's separation remains a mystery. They may meet and begin to redevelop pair bonds during their travels north. They may wait and not unite until after they arrive at the nesting lake. Males seem to arrive first. If the pair is newly formed, the male apparently attracts the female to the nesting home (or vice versa, if the female arrives first).

Regardless of how loon pairs meet each spring, their nesting lake provides a stage for their nuptial displays. These displays serve as ceremonies to bond the pair together for the

summer's challenge of rearing young.

The first subtle displays of pairing and courtship take place early in the season on the waters that the loons claim as their nesting territory. If you are lucky, you might find a situation where such loons become comfortable with your presence near them. If so, on a still and

This loon is in the middle of a wing flap.

◀ *Loons fly in a wing-tip to wing-tip formation, calling the tremolo..*

excited dives and body shakes, erupting into a wild series of splashing wing flaps, as the birds rush across the water propelled by their wings.

The first sign of a pair of loons that have bonded might, however, come later. You might see a tandem flight of two loons in tight formation, wing to wing, circling over the lake. They may make a call or two as they fly. If the loons then set their wings into a V-shape, high above their backs, and drop in a curving steep glide, watch where they land together on the lake.

Where they land gives an important message to other loons. They proclaim for all who care to watch that the place where they have landed is now their home. It is where they intend to nest. And they will defend their home turf. You can bet that any other loons within sight distance have taken note of this display.

quiet day you may hear much chatter between them as they court and establish their bond. They swim toward each other with bills toward the sky and heads turning side to side. Then they rapidly dip their bills into the water and shake them side to side. This might escalate into a series of short,

Other Displays

The most dramatic loon displays are performed when they sense danger to their nest or to their young from an intruder to their territory. They will stretch their necks up high and ride high in the water, swimming with clear deliberation directly toward the threat. Both the male and female may join in. Rapid swimming, with great splashing of thrashing wings, may come next. Their displays then grow in excitement.

In its most dramatic form, this display may culminate in the loon's fascinating "penguin," or water, dance. One loon or both will rear up on the surface of the water, breast and neck thrust high, and run upright across the water, splashing and dancing as they go, often accompanying the dance with a series of tremolo calls. They may race this way, singly or as a pair, for up to a quarter-mile, circling around and returning to near their

▶ *Watch a loon's body language as you approach, and back away if it appears to become more alert.*

starting point. This flurry of activity can even lead to the loons becoming airborne.

As fascinating as this display may be, it's a sign that the loons are suffering great agitation caused by their discomfort with an intruder. Should that intruder ever be you, leave the area at once, for the loon is losing precious time and energy in defending its territory or young against you. The more a loon's attention is directed away from feeding and the care of young, the greater the chance the summer's nesting season will fail. While the parents are preoccupied with intruding humans, the chicks are left alone, vulnerable to predators or other threats and not receiving the food they need in this critical season of growth.

The many exuberant displays and interactions between loons serve two purposes. First, they strengthen the strong bond between the pair, ensuring a commitment through the challenging weeks ahead of nesting and of rearing chicks. Both adults must help with these arduous ordeals.

Second, these courtship displays inform neighboring and prospecting loons that a strongly committed pair has taken possession of that portion of the lake and that the territory will be defended. That message, given through sight and sound, lessens the need for confrontations and saves much wear and tear within the community of loons.

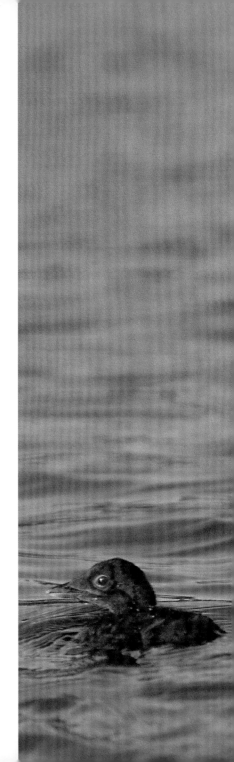

▲ *These two loons are copulating, which they rarely do at a nest site.*

The loons send a message to you as well with these displays, one that tells you two things. First, their message says that you are lucky to know that the lake holds interest to a nesting pair of loons. Second, by the specific location of their displays, the loons have told you the section of the lake they have chosen as their territory. You now know where they will nest, raise their young, and defend against intruders. You know where to focus your observations. And you know the special place that needs your help for protection and stewardship, so that these loons can return to it each spring.

Nesting

Two to three weeks of courtship displaying pass before the female lays her first egg, when incubation begins. The level of the water in the nesting lake plays a significant role in determining the starting date for nesting. Snow melt and the rains of spring bring flood waters that often keep the shore-edged nesting sites of loons submerged during their first several weeks on the lake. By the time that the water level drops and nesting sites emerge and dry out, the birds have formed strong pair bonds. Actual mating, a brief and seldom seen moment, takes place. Within a matter of days, the female goes ashore to lay her eggs.

Nesting sites are special. The same sites may be used year after year and by generation after generation of loons. Individual loons and mated pairs will commonly return to at least try to use the same nest site each year.

It also appears that young birds, once they've reached breeding age at six or seven, frequently return to the lakes of their birth to begin their own search for nesting grounds. In this way, loons may establish family neighborhoods on surrounding lakes. Competition is strong for nest sites and for mates, however, and one or both loons of a pair might be replaced from year to year within a nesting territory.

Common loons always nest next to water. This is a necessity, since loons are unable to walk on land. They need to be able to swim to the edge of their nests, then with little effort position themselves onto the nest.

Being close to water also provides a quick and easy escape for loons. They are highly vulnerable when out of water and are constantly on the watch

▲ *Common loons typically lay two eggs. Here, one of the two has already hatched.*

of a marshy stream, elevated only an inch or two above the water surface. The ground where the eggs are laid is often still wet. While loons add little vegetation to the nest before the eggs are laid, they often add it as they incubate the eggs. In that way, the nest gains in bulk through the coming weeks.

Eggs and Incubation

Loons most often lay two eggs. Some lay only one and, rarely, they may lay three. A day or two separates the laying of each egg.

Incubation begins with the laying of the first egg. A staggered start results in different hatching dates for the chicks. Incubation takes an average of 27-29 days, with the eggs attended almost continually, day and night, through that time. Both the male and the female loon share in the incubation duties.

for predators of other signs of danger. Loons always choose nest sites with water deep enough for a submerged escape near the nest's edge.

Common loons make their nests from not much other than bare earth or some hastily matted vegetation, and with little preparation other than the scraping of a slight depression to hold the eggs. They may build their nest on an island's shore or on floating vegetation at the edge

The average time a loon sits on the eggs before exchanging with its mate ranges from four to six hours. During rainy or stormy nights the nest duty may require a longer stint. A loon may also sit for longer periods during the last few days before the chicks hatch.

The incubating bird passes time quietly, always alert for danger. It may occasionally pull loose vegetation that it finds within reach to add to the nest, and it will stand and reposition itself and the eggs every hour or so. Otherwise, the bird sits quite still. It always sits facing the water to observe all that approaches. That position also permits a quick escape if needed.

A loon will occasionally nap while incubating, nodding off for just a few moments. When the loon is ready to exchange duties, it calls to its mate. If the mate isn't near, the bird will call repeatedly and loudly until the mate responds. When its mate arrives near the nest, the

incubating bird quietly slips into the water and swims away to feed, stretch, or preen.

The new incubating parent goes immediately to the nest, rearranges the eggs, perhaps adds to or rearranges the nesting material and then settles down on the eggs. The warmth from the

▲ *This parent is rearranging the egg before settling down for a turn at incubation.*

▲ *Loon chicks pass their first weeks in quiet sheltered waters under the watchful eyes of their parents.*

adult's body pressed against the eggs sustains the embryo inside and stimulates its growth.

Loon Chicks

The adults can hear and feel the chicks inside the eggs during the days just before they hatch. The first laid egg usually hatches first. A day or two might separate the hatching of each egg.

The chicks have a coat of soft black down when they hatch. They are quite wet from hatching, and it takes several hours for them to dry and for the down to fluff up into a warm, protective coat.

A loon chick can walk and swim right after it hatches, and just as soon as it dries off, the chick will start exploring the perimeter and surroundings of the nest, even while the adult may still sit on an unhatched egg. A loon chick, however, never wanders out of its parents' watchful gaze.

One of the adult loons may call the chick to water within a few hours after hatching. If another egg requires tending, the loons might shelter the hatched chick beneath them until the other chick emerges, perhaps even overnight. Once the last chick has hatched and dried, all will leave the nest. Most never return to the nest that year because of their vulnerability on land.

Loons are extremely attentive parents. They never leave their newly hatched young alone. A chick passes its first weeks in quiet sheltered

▲ *Loon chicks soon learn their parents' behavior of peering beneath the surface.*

waters, always with at least one parent near its side, while the other fishes or keeps watch not far away.

The chicks can swim ably from the time of their hatch. And immediately upon entering the water, they begin the loon's habit of peering underwater.

They also have a natural inclination to dive, even when only a few days old. A newly hatched chick finds diving difficult, however, being covered with a mass of soft, buoyant down. They can get just beneath the surface before they pop up like a

cork. They soon give up trying until they're older and stronger, when their first feathers begin to replace the down.

By instinct, newly hatched loon chicks climb aboard a parent's back when in the water. This wonderful adaptation for survival, where their parent's back replaces the nest they left while still so young, offers a warm platform upon which to rest and to sleep. It also provides a safe haven from predators lurking below. Bass, pickerel and muskie would enjoy a meal of an unprotected baby loon.

▶ *A loon chick will ride on one of its parents' backs during its first couple of weeks, perhaps longer.*

A chance encounter with a family of loons serenely swimming by with a chick tucked snugly and safely on one of the parents' backs makes an endearing northwoods sight that will stay with you forever. If you have patience, you may even get to see one of the parents feeding a chick while it rides on the other's back.

Both adults participate in the constant care for and feeding of their chicks. And the young are ravenous! They need a constant supply of food to fuel their rapid growth. Loon chicks attain close to adult size in just three months. And from a weight of just a few ounces at hatching, they grow to be nearly equal that of an adult loon by the time that they first fly from their birth lake.

▲ *Both loon parents assist in raising their young.*

Food for these young birds includes small fish, just an inch or two long, and small aquatic insects such as dragonfly larvae. The adults catch the food for the chicks and present it to them while held in their bills. The youngsters take the food and swallow it whole, even when just a few days old. When an excited young chick accidentally drops the offered food, the adult will patiently retrieve it and present it again.

As a loon chick grows, the size of the food brought by its parents increases in size as well. Chicks also become more aggressive and swim to meet their parents as they arrive with food.

The parents soon make the chicks work more

▲ *Offerings to chicks include small fish.*

for their food. They start by holding the food away from the chick, requiring it to reach and grab at the food, thereby improving its aim and coordination. They also begin to drop the food, often stunned but still alive, in the water as the chick approaches. This teaches the chick to catch and retrieve its own food. You sometimes see an adult dive several times to retrieve a fish missed by its chick. They will continue to bring the fish back and drop it near the chick, time after time, until the chick succeeds.

As a loon chick matures, it grows in its ability to catch its own food. Newly hatched chicks already peck at and occasionally catch small insects and bits of vegetation floating on the surface. A chick's adeptness develops quickly, and by the time it is two months old, a loon chick can regularly catch food on its own. Its parents will continue to bring it food until it can fly, however. And the chick will not refuse any offerings; loon young are persistent beggars.

As new hatchlings, loon chicks talk to their parents with soft squeaks and peeps. Older chicks squeak and peep like young chickens when they

beg for food from their parents. This communication continues all through the summer and is a wonderful thing to hear if you can gain the confidence of a family of loons and be allowed to share that pleasure. A chick in late summer, by then nearly a full-sized bird capable of fishing on its own, seems quite odd and out-of-place when seen begging with such calls.

You can estimate the age of loon chicks from their size and shape as they grow through the summer. A chick no bigger than a tennis ball and still round in shape is probably less than ten days, possibly no more than a week old. By three weeks

of age, a chick becomes larger than a softball, with a hint of a stretch to its length. At five or six weeks old, a chick looks about the size of a football. And by the time it is ten weeks old a chick approaches a size equal to an adult loon.

The feathering and colors of loon chicks can also help you guess their age. For their first two weeks, chicks wear the dark, sooty colored down they had at hatching. By four weeks old, that has been replaced by a second coat of down, this one rich brown in color. That down is gradually replaced by their full set of juvenile feathers by eight weeks, which they will wear through the

▲ *Clockwise from left to right: a day-old loon chick rides parent's back; at 3 weeks, still covered in down; at 4.5 weeks, when back feathers begin to grow; and at 6 weeks, when the chick's plumage is nearly all gray feathers (opposite page).*

coming winter. The first signs of these whitish colored feathers showing through the down indicate a chick of five weeks of age. By eight weeks of age, the last remnants of this down cling in a motley form atop the loon's head and back.

Young loons can fly when about three months old. While some may make their first flight as early as their tenth or eleventh week, twelve weeks seems to be the average age when real flying begins. With the average date of hatching being in late June into early July throughout most of the common loon's range, you can expect the young to be flying by September or October.

Late-hatchers face the threat that an early ice-up of their birth lake might prevent them from leaving if they do not learn to fly while adequate water remains open to provide the long runway that a loon needs to get airborne. The rare loon that waits too long to leave is doomed.

The Calls of Loons:
Understanding What You Hear

The wailing call arouses you from a deep sleep in the camp on the shore of a wondrous lake in the northwoods. The voice sounds again: the gentle but forceful call of a loon on the far end of the wooded lake. The haunting, wailing call lulls you half-awake even as it makes a soothing lullaby for a perfect end to a perfect day.

Soon a change in the call arouses your senses even more. Then a second call, that of a more distant voice, responds to the first loon. Now a third caller joins in the midnight chorus!

Enthralled by the boreal trio, you lay listening to their conversations.

The distance and direction of the three calls says that they come from three different lakes. The first comes from a loon on the lake you share, the others from neighboring lakes beyond the nearby hills, one to the east, one to the south. What a magical and mysterious moment to experience, this still clear night with the stars brilliant against the black sky, and the only sounds to be heard are the calling of the three loons to one another.

▶ *Lakes with loons often come alive after the sun goes down.*

You wonder what they were saying and why. Was there a special message that they shared? Or did they simply sing for joy? While pondering these questions, you feel honored to be part of the nocturnal connection amongst these wild creatures.

That midnight chorus awakens a realization that you don't need to see a loon to appreciate the special part that they play as you experience the natural world. It reveals just how much enjoyment you can gain and what insights you can attain by paying attention to what you hear—even of loons unseen—as well as what you see. It also demonstrates how a better understanding of the biology, behavior and habitat of loons greatly enhances your enjoyment when you hear them.

▲ *A male loon does a crouch yodel as he defends his chick from the approach of another loon.*

Why They Call

The calls of loons have been described as haunting, mysterious, enthralling, and enchanting. Their calls resonating through the night are sounds never to be forgotten for those fortunate enough to hear their conversation, and are to many a wild music that symbolizes the very essence of the northwoods.

Loons call to communicate with others of their kind. They communicate with several basic types of call. Researchers and loon watchers have labeled these as the tremolo, the wail, the yodel, and what might best be described as quiet chatter. Using these basic types of calls, loons also create variations, sometimes combining parts of each. For example, loons often employ the tremolo sung in combination with a wail or in combination with a yodel.

They also create variations by stringing several calls of one type together. And they occasionally vary the number of individual notes within each type of call. Each combination and variation no doubt sends a slightly different message.

Their creativity at times seems almost endless, especially when more than a single loon joins in the chorus. You will never be bored from repetition by the calls of a chorus of loons. The vast array of their orchestrations displays a hallmark of their nature; the creativity of their communication is difficult to find surpassed. Do loons

somehow view the northern lakes as auditoriums? Perhaps at times they sing as much for pleasure as to communicate.

The Wail

A mournful, drawn-out sounding call somewhat reminiscent of a wolf howl, the wail is made in an almost infinite variety of forms, each with apparently a subtle change in meaning. Loons almost always employ the wail in all its forms as a call of greeting or searching for another loon, usually to a mate or a chick.

A loon incubating eggs on the nest will wail to its mate that may be out of sight elsewhere on the lake when it wants to exchange places. Loons also use the wail to contact a mate that has temporarily gone to a nearby lake to feed or to explore.

Loons use the wail to maintain contact. They also shorten this call to a "hoot," which they use as a greeting when returning to each other or to call

at hand, the throat of a bird making the wail call can be seen to expand and contract like a croaking frog.

The Tremolo

A string of abrupt, high and low notes, the tremolo sounds akin to mad laughter. The tremolo often serves as an alarm call. It is one call that a loon watcher must learn to respect, for if it's given as you approach, the loon's clear message should be heeded: "You've come too close to my space." The bird has reacted negatively to your presence. You need to back off and rethink your loon watching plans.

Perhaps you've gone too far too fast with your approach. Even though the bird may be swimming away from you while giving the tremolo alarm, you need to leave as well. You may have invaded an area important to the loon. There may be a chick hidden nearby, or eggs in a nest. Your

out to their chicks hidden in shoreline vegetation during the parent's absence. When given with a sharp, abrupt edge to it or in a series of quick calls, the hoot may also serve as an alarm to their chicks or to a mate that danger exists nearby.

Softer versions of the wail are often used in quieter, more private conversations between loons, especially mated pairs. Lucky observers may hear such private conversations when trustful loons swim nearby. When observed close

presence puts them in jeopardy. That loon has just given a message to you in loon language.

The tremolo is often heard at night. Although yodels, wails and tremolos are all used in the nighttime serenades, the tremolo is considered the most common, especially in duets or choruses.

The tremolo is also the only call given in flight. A single flying bird may give this call, and listen for a response from a friend or stranger on the lake below. A particularly beautiful sound is that of a pair of flying loons singing the tremolo in duet. The action of their beating wings and accompanying body motion adds an extra,

rhythmic nature to this call while in flight.

The tremolo may be used by flying birds to stay in contact with their young on a lake below. While taking photographs for this book, Bill Silliker watched a group of four adult loons repeatedly fly around a lake, calling out the tremolo. They gave every appearance on that September day to be calling to several young loons on the lake below, enticing those birds yet to have flown to test their recently grown feathers, to try a maiden flight and

▶ *The tremolo call is the only one made by loons in flight.*

join them as they circled the lake in preparation for the fall migration soon to come.

The Yodel

Only the male loon makes the yodel call. The yodel may signal serious aggression when used by the male in establishing its territory in the spring or in defending it against intruders through the summer nesting months.

Loons often call with the yodel at dusk and early morning, usually in a repeated series of five or six calls. When not used as part of a reaction to a challenge to the territory, the yodel may announce that the owner of that spot has come home. It is often given by the male when alone in this more relaxed setting.

The yodel also serves as part of the mating and bonding ritual of a breeding pair during the establishment of their nesting territory. In this use, often at dawn or dusk, the male often carries

on with an enthusiastic series of yodels. Other males may join in, calling from their own nearby territories.

Quiet Chatter

When calm and undisturbed, loons communicate with one another using a variety of quiet calls. The sounds have been described, by those close enough to hear, as everything from chirps to peeps, from mews to squeaks, and even quiet hoots. These sounds combine at times to form an

▲ *This loon is at the end of a wing flap.*

▶ *This loon is in the midst of a wing flap/preening shake.*

almost constant chatter between a pair of loons, between parents or chicks, or among a flock of gathered loons. Time and quiet patience may bring you within a private circle of loons communicating this way, perhaps even with a loon gently greeting its chick or the chick calling as it begs for food. Strive for such opportunities—you will not regret your efforts.

Learning the Calls

The most pleasurable way to learn the calls of the loon is to spend some time on a lake in nesting country and work to distinguish one call from the others as you listen. Commercially available recordings provide a helpful aid to that approach. A number of high quality tapes, records and CDs sold by local Audubon groups, nature centers, bird feed stores and other loon conservation groups provide descriptive narratives of the various loon calls to help you understand what you hear.

Such recorded aids provide wonderful guides for learning the language of loons. They also permit you to develop your skills during times when it's impossible to visit a northern lake. And they offer a perfect respite during a cold and snowy winter's night.

Individual Voices

The wonders of "loon talk" don't end with just these several different types of calls, even when loons splice them together. Through careful listening and study, we now know that individual loons each have their own distinctive voice. Just as we recognize the individual, distinctive voice of each person that we meet, we can also recognize individual loons by the characteristics of their voices and calls.

By the time a chick has reached the end of its first summer, it gains the voice of an adolescent and has probably already obtained a distinctive voice. It uses a set of calls—a language and a dialect—all its own that it will employ throughout life. Without a doubt, these variations enable loons to recognize their mates, their young and their neighbors, and permit them to identify strangers.

Our ears are not well enough attuned to distinguish these subtle variations. Researchers have identified these fascinating distinctions by the analysis of sound recordings. The patterns of amplitude and frequency clearly show the unique quality of each loon's voice.

Although sophisticated, the equipment to record and study the calls of loons has become increasingly affordable and available in recent years. An advanced loon watcher armed with this gear might even be able to look for these variations and perhaps start to recognize individual loons by their voices.

▶ *Loon chicks peep to communicate to their parents.*

CHAPTER SIX

Photographing Loons

The common loon presents an uncommon challenge for the wildlife photographer: how to capture the two extremes of light reflectance, pure white and nearly pure black, with a single exposure setting. Even worse, the dark red eye on the common loon doesn't record well on film unless light hits it fairly straight on. In wildlife photography, if you've missed the eye, you've usually missed it all.

Most of what we record on film is reflected light. The brightness of that reflected light varies due to both the texture of the objects that we photograph and the wavelength, or the color, of the light reflected by those objects. White appearing objects reflect all colors well, and therefore, lots of light. Black appearing objects reflect little, if any light. Anyone who doubts that need only point their camera's exposure meter at a white light reflecting object and then toward a black light reflecting object in the same light. Your meter will detect a wide range of reflectance.

How much reflectance film can record depends

◀ *Photographing loons requires an understanding of film exposure.*

▶ *Autofocus can help to capture action moments, such as this loon that is in the middle of a head scratch.*

on its latitude. Color negative films, the ones we get snapshots on in print form, have a wide range of latitude. Black-and-white films also have a good deal of latitude. Because of that, both types of film forgive mistakes in setting the exposure when you take a photograph. Your photolab can pull a reasonable print out of either color negative film or black-and-white film even if you erred by as much as two exposure settings—usually called "stops"—too bright or too dark from what would be a perfect setting.

Color slide film has much less latitude. In fact, slide film cannot properly record more than a

"stop" off of a perfect exposure setting. Miss by more than that and the colors are either all washed out looking (overexposure), or too dark to show any detail (underexposure). Even so, professional nature photographers shoot mostly slide film, because that's what most magazines and books require from which to publish.

The answer to this difficulty is to set your exposure for the detail that's most important. With a common loon, that's the white. If you expose for the black, which doesn't show much detail to begin with, you'll "blow out" the white so badly that it may actually look blurred.

Setting Up

When setting up for loon photography, first set your camera as if to photograph an object of average reflectance by metering off of green grass or, preferably, from an "18-percent gray" card purchased from a camera store. All camera meters are calibrated to record the light reflecting from a "gray" card as an average exposure.

Next, adjust the exposure setting to allow one-half to perhaps two-thirds of a "stop" less light to reach the film, depending on how bright the light is that's hitting the loon. While this underexposes the black head of the loon and can make the water around a loon a bit darker than you might normally expose for, it keeps the white from blowing out and ruining the picture.

And how to capture the eye? As previously mentioned, the red eye doesn't reflect well unless light is hitting it pretty straight on. Light early in the morning or late in the afternoon strikes the

place you're on at a low angle, as the sun rises and sets. Light at such a low angle hits a loon right smack in the eye.

That light is also softer and not nearly as brightly reflective as the light when the sun is higher in the sky. That's a plus for loon photography, because softer light reflects more photogenically off of the white.

▲   *A low light angle makes it easier to catch the red eye of a common loon on film.*

▲ *Never approach too closely to a nesting loon, and stop at any signs of disturbance.*

Capturing a Loon on Film

You also need to know how to get close enough to a loon for photography without harassing it. The first thing to do is to study a loon's behavior from a respectful distance. Watch especially how it reacts to people in boats or canoes nearby. Some loons are more habituated to seeing people in watercraft and don't get alarmed—unless you charge up on them in a direct approach. Please never do that.

You should never interfere with or approach too closely to a nesting loon. Most jurisdictions have laws against the harassment of loons, especially at nest sites and "nursery" areas, the sheltered coves and inlets where the parents stay with newly hatched chicks. Some lakes even have loon wardens who monitor breeding loons to protect them from interference. While respecting the rules of any particular place not only makes good sense, respect for the needs of your subjects makes even better sense.

Professional wildlife photographers use long telephoto lenses to capture special moments with

subjects as sensitive as nesting loons. While some of the nesting loon images in this book were made from only seventy-five feet away, the approach to these special, habituated loons often took hours and required constant vigilance for any signs of alarm or distress.

It's also worth noting that this photographer worked with loons at remote ponds where few others go to attempt to capture them on film. An absence of human numbers always makes for less pressure on wildlife subjects. Had the nesting loons been at lakes frequented by people regularly trying to photograph them, these photo sessions might well have been approached differently. Remember that cumulative impacts can occur on wild subjects.

Always watch your subject for any indication that it is uneasy because of your approach. You should be aware of your distance from loons at all times as you watch their body language to ensure that your presence does not affect their behavior. Learn the signs that a loon makes when it does get alarmed. If a loon displays by spreading its wings or if it calls out with a tremolo as you

This photographer has earned the trust of the loon he is photographing by floating with the breeze.

approach, it's probably telling you that your actions have disturbed it. Back off. And if it gets up on its feet in a "penguin dance," you've definitely upset it. Get out of there immediately.

Never approach a loon in a straight non-stop method. A successful technique is to stop the canoe or boat at a comfortable distance for the loon. Then simply float with the wind or current toward the loon. After a while, the loon may actually approach on its own. Loons are very curious animals. Sometimes when you let a loon set a distance it is comfortable with, you just might be surprised how relaxed it will become in your presence. That's when you and your subject both win.

And you get to photograph magic while in the presence of loons.

CHAPTER SEVEN

Loon Conservation

Any definition or description of the essence of loons as living creatures would be incomplete without an appreciation of their past, for their ancestral lineage is old and exclusive. It is exclusive because just five living species of loons exist in the world, a small number when compared to other groups of birds.

While the five loon species are closely related to each other, they are distant relatives from other living birds. Researchers have to go back about twenty-five million years before finding connec-

tions to other lines of living birds. And on the loon branch of the bird family tree, only a few other forms of loons—all now extinct—are known to have existed. It is remarkable that with such a narrow line of evolution a species could survive so relatively unchanged for such a long time. This is truly a defining testament to the creation that we call the loon, especially when taking into consideration the monumental changes on a worldwide, geologic, and evolutionary scale that have occurred during those millions of years. It is

◀ *The loon has evolved over millions of years, making it one of the oldest of surviving bird species.*

a wonder that the lineage of loons has been able to survive and succeed through it all.

Loons as we know them today have existed for at least twenty million years! Humans have only walked this earth for perhaps three to four million years—merely a fifth of that time.

The loon, therefore, has successfully completed twenty million annual migrations from nesting to wintering grounds. Loons have succeeded in rais-

ing the next generation twenty million times. Loons have filled summer nights with their ancient, wailing calls for twenty million years.

The changes loons have witnessed and needed to adjust to have been monumental through those years. Glaciers have come and gone numerous times, burying the land under miles of ice; eliminating, and then reforming traditional loon nesting lakes. Sea levels have risen and fallen, completely reshaping tried and tested migration travel routes and obliterating ancient winter homes and sources of food.

Around them, other species with which they existed and perhaps depended on have disappeared from the face of the earth, unable to cope with the drastically changing world. Yet amidst all this, loons have persisted remarkably unchanged,

a testament to the success of their original evolutionary design. Is it any wonder then, that the loon has such a special hold on our hearts and spirits?

What of today, however? The safety and shelter of the special lakes which have protected and sustained loons through so many nesting seasons may not last another century. Loons face a new challenge: the challenge of humans and our activities. People are arriving on these once remote lakes in ever greater numbers. Picnic areas now attract predators to the very sites that sheltered loons from them for centuries. Camps and even year-round homes dot the shores of ancient nesting waters. Shores that never saw a wave, being sheltered in the lee of islands or coves, are now awash each summer with the wakes of motorboats and jet skis. And in their wakes, nesting sites that have withstood the test of thousands of years have disappeared. Clear, clean waters that have provided a healthy environment and food for millions of years are now increasingly contaminated with mercury and other pollutants, products of our industrialization. Lost, broken or discarded lead sinkers used by anglers (ingested by loons

with the gravel they need to grind their food) are poisonous—and are now the number one cause of death for these wonderful birds.

The test today is not only for loons to adapt to the pressures we humans put upon them, but a test for us as well. Can we understand the needs of loons? Do we have the will to balance our use of these special lakes and waters?

If we degrade these special sites by our actions—through pollution, contamination, by filling, dredging, development, or by levels of activity and disturbances by people beyond what loons can withstand—where will the loons go? There are but a limited number of sites providing the necessities for loons and those sites already support all the loons that they can hold.

Keep in mind what these special, traditionally used sites tell us from the loon's perspective. They tell us that our coasts and lakes are not all the same. They tell us that only certain waters and locations provide the right mix of the things that loons need to survive. They tell us that when any of these special sites are lost, then the number of loons will decline. Local populations can be lost entirely in this way, and if such losses become a trend, entire populations might be jeopardized.

After loons have succeeded against truly mon-

▲ *The loss of the use of ancient breeding habitat due to human interference threatens the future of loons.*

does it say about us if we cannot manage human affairs in our time so that a way of life that has existed for roughly fifty million years could continue?

You can help loons to survive. Build relationships with the landowners around the loon watching sites that you discover. Work with them and with local and state conservation groups to help educate others about the needs of loons. Support conservation efforts such as the Adopt-A-Loon Project of the Biodiversity Research Institute (www.loonmagic.com) and efforts to protect special loon habitats.

umental changes on a global scale, are we humans now presenting them with challenges they might not survive? What would that mean for us and for other forms of life, if a creature as proven and successful as the loon could not withstand the changes we are now bringing to this planet? What

We owe that much to the loons that have so enthralled us. And if not to the loons, then to our own future generations—who undoubtedly will also seek the peace and the connection to the natural world that one finds in the presence of loons.